Experiential Knowledge

Understanding Our Journey Into Relationship With God

Mark Calvin Nelson

Sword of the Spirit Publishing

ISBN 13: **978-1-9392192-6-8**

www.swordofspirit.net

Dedication

I would like to dedicate this
book to my beloved son
Luke. I am so glad and
proud that you are my son.
You make me so happy!
You are truly a special boy,
and funny too. I love your
heart for music and
adventure. I love watching
your toughness, resilience,
and resolute heart. You will
always be my Lukey baby!

Introduction

Think about the times in your life that are the most significant and life-changing. Do they involve excitement? Were there moments of risk and danger? If you are an adrenaline junkie like me, some of the hallmark times in your life involve all of the above. The times that have captivated me and changed me forever were moments where the experience was beyond my ability to describe.

Some of the most significant things that happen to us spiritually are truly indescribable, but the mark left on our life is indelible. My conversion to a life lived for God was significant. I remember how difficult it was trying to explain to my family and friends what had happened to me when Jesus came into my life. A lot of them looked at me with confusion wondering if I had lost my mind because my story sounded like this: "Jesus came into my heart and I was crying and laughing at the same time. I had such grief and such peace. I felt so convicted and so free. I felt so afraid and so loved. I didn't want what I was experiencing to end, but I knew that if I continued, I would run out of tears and snot, and I was laughing so hard my stomach hurt." This story didn't win a lot of converts at first, but the changed person that I was, did. It was almost as though the story of my encounter reached into the hearts of those who heard it and pulled on their hearts for such an experience. I believe that God made the human heart for encounters.

As you read this book, may your heart fill up with the awe and wonder of who God is for you, and may your understanding grow in anticipation of experiencing the heights and depths of His great love for you (Ephesians 3:18).

Chapter 1

Biblical Knowledge

It seems to be a distinguishing factor for someone to introduce themselves as an intellectual Christian, but it's a dig if someone in the faith is considered to be an emotional, encounter-driven Christian. Why? Can't emotional, encounter-driven Christians be strong intellectually, or is it that intellectual Christians can't seem to get out of their own heads and encounter God? I believe both assessments fall short of His glory so to speak. I would like to look at scripture in the original language to try to bring clarity and encounter.

Kris Vallotton says, *"Your heart can take you places your head can't go."* In my opinion, there is a lot of truth to that statement. Thankfully our heart is capable of receiving revelation and experience before our brain. If we are led by our brain we'll talk ourselves out of what God is trying to thrust us into. In your physical body, truth travels due north. Truth is revealed and received into our hearts. It is with the heart we believe (Romans 10:10). Scripture *doesn't* say that it's with the brain we believe. 2 Corinthians 3 tells us that when we are in Jesus, the veil that covers our heart is taken away and we now have permission to contemplate the Lord's glory and be transformed into His image. These things are an activity of the heart.

We live in a culture that exalts academia. The quest for academic knowledge is instilled into all of us from

early in our childhood
development. I would like
to say the hunger to learn is
right, but the need to know
everything is wrong. We
walk by faith not
understanding. We are not
responsible to know
everything, except what He
reveals to us through
revelation. Factual
information about the
scripture will not change our
life. A strong intellect is not
an indicator of strong faith.
However, the hunger of the
righteous to learn and to get
revelation will not be
denied; those who hunger

will be filled; those who seek will find.

We glorify those who have a strong intellectual and cognitive ability. We praise logic and reason. It is ingrained in us to live rationally; so here's where it gets hairy. God isn't logical or rational!

The academic study of scripture *doesn't* have the power to transform our life. No matter how many Bible verses we memorize, our heart has the potential to be unchanged.

God is full of wisdom, creativity, and imagination.

We walk with God in trust not understanding. Proverbs 3:5-6 is a favorite passage for many. *"Trust in the Lord with all your HEART, and lean not to your own UNDERSTANDING; In all your ways acknowledge Him, and He shall direct your paths."* Trust and understanding don't go together. If we plan on following our understanding, we're in big trouble. We were meant to walk with God through wisdom, revelation and experience, not logic, reason and understanding. The heart is where revelation occurs. Wisdom is the result of revelation. Biblical understanding comes to our heart, not our head.

<u>Hebrews 11:3</u> says, *"<u>By faith we understand</u> that the universe was formed at God's command, so that what is seen was not made out of what was visible."* Faith precedes understanding.

<u>Psalms 49:3</u>

My mouth shall speak wisdom, And the meditation of my heart shall give understanding.

Information shared to someone without a personal

revelation results in human reasoning or head knowledge, not true Biblical understanding. If we are going to choose human reasoning then we are limited to human resource. We like being reasonable because we can reason our way out of doing anything. This is not wisdom.

Many confuse wisdom and logic. In fact, some use logic and reason to excuse Biblical responsibility. This is not who we are, and that is not fun! With His revelation, we are learning to be led by our heart's trust into understanding and wisdom.

We didn't get saved in our heads – it's with the heart we believe (Romans 10:9). When we read the scripture, the one thing that stands out above all is that we can't have a cerebral relationship with God and experience Him.

Most of the things God does don't make sense; that's why we can only experience Him supernaturally. We can't experience God logically. In fact, the Bible isn't even logical. The gospel isn't logical. Half of the stuff that God does *doesn't* make sense to our natural reasoning mind.

Here's the kicker – the person, dealings, revelations, and encounters of God make perfect sense to our hearts. Revelation happens in the heart and the Holy Spirit is kind and faithful to give us understanding later. Even the knowledge mentioned in the New Testament is an experiential knowledge first and an intellectual knowledge second.

What does knowledge mean? Acquaintance with facts, truths, or principles, as from study or investigation. When you hear the word knowledge what do you think? Where is knowledge? How do we get knowledge?

There are two different Greek words for knowledge I would like to discuss – we actually need both. The first word for knowledge is *gnosis*. This knowledge speaks of intellectual, head, and scientific knowledge. *Gnosis* knowledge speaks of lawful, principal knowledge[1].

The second word for knowledge is *epignosis*. This knowledge is defined as the correct knowledge of divine things [2]. In other words, it is an experiential knowledge. Ephesians 1:17-20 says, *"That the God of our Lord Jesus Christ, the Father of glory, may give to you the spirit of wisdom and revelation in the knowledge (epignosis) of Him, the eyes of your understanding being enlightened; that you may know (see) what is the hope of His calling, what are the riches of the glory of His inheritance in the saints, and what is the exceeding greatness of His power toward us who believe, according to the working of His mighty power which He worked in Christ when He raised Him from the dead*

*and seated Him at His right
hand in the heavenly
places."*

The verb for knowledge is
ginosko, which is translated
as an experience of coming
into, perceiving, feeling,
acquainting with, and it is
the Jewish expression for
intimacy between man and
woman. This word is used
223 times in the New
Testament. It is what is
beyond or as a result of
knowledge [3].

Ephesians 3:17-19 uses it
this way, *"That Christ may
dwell in your hearts through
faith; that you, being rooted
and grounded in love, may*

be able to comprehend with all the saints what is the width and length and depth and height-- to know (ginosko) the love of Christ which passes knowledge (gnosis); that you may be filled with all the fullness of God."

Paul is praying that the church in Ephesus would come to know Christ better. How? Through a spirit of wisdom and revelation. Paul is saying that encounter and experience are our greatest tools to know God's love. We know the incomparable great power of God experientially not academically.

In other words, the experience of knowledge in our hearts through experienced intimacy is meant to surpass our head knowledge of academia. The critical point is that the experience of our identity is a heart affair and an encounter, not strictly an intellectual, scientific understanding. So actually, we are led by our heart, but we still need our brain.

2 Peter 1:5-9

"But also for this very reason, giving all diligence, add to your faith virtue, to virtue knowledge, 6 to

knowledge self-control, to self-control perseverance, to perseverance godliness, 7 to godliness brotherly kindness, and to brotherly kindness love. 8 For if these things are yours and abound, you will be neither barren nor unfruitful in the knowledge of our Lord Jesus Christ. 9 For he who lacks these things is shortsighted, even to blindness, and has forgotten that he was cleansed from his old sins."

Have you ever ridden a roller coaster? There are two relationships that you can have with a roller coaster. First, you could intellectually study the roller coaster. There is a lot of factually fascinating information that can be gathered about a roller coaster. The physics is quite complicated. Have you ever wondered how you can cruise down a track at sixty miles an hour in a cart that has no engine? The car is pulled to the top of the first hill at the beginning of the ride, but after that the coaster must complete the ride on its own. You aren't being propelled around the track by a motor or pulled by a hitch. The conversion of potential energy to kinetic energy is what drives the roller coaster; and all of the kinetic energy you need for the ride is present once the coaster descends the first hill. Once you're underway, different types of wheels help keep the ride smooth. Running wheels guide the coaster on the track. Friction wheels control lateral motion (movement to either side of the track). A final set of wheels keeps the coaster on the track even if it's inverted. Compressed air brakes stop the car as the ride ends. The physics of a roller coaster is as follows: Gravitational potential energy is greatest at the highest point of a roller coaster and least at the lowest point. Kinetic energy is energy an object has because of its motion and is equal to one-half multiplied by the mass of an object multiplied by its velocity squared (KE = 1/2 mv2).

The vocabulary of physics that affect roller coaster riders are as follows:

acceleration: How quickly an object speeds up, slows down or changes direction. Is equal to change in velocity divided by time.

critical velocity: The speed needed at the top of a loop for a car to make it through the loop without falling off the track.

force: Any push or pull.

friction: A force caused by a rubbing motion between two objects.

g-force: Short for gravitational force. The force exerted on an object by the Earth's gravity at sea level.

gravitational constant: The acceleration caused by Earth's gravity at sea level. Is equal to 9.81 m/sec^2 (32.2 ft/sec^2).

gravity: A force that draws any two objects toward one another.

kinetic energy: The energy of an object in motion, which is directly related to its velocity and its mass.

potential energy: The energy stored by an object ready to be used. (In this lesson, we use gravitational potential energy, which is directly related to the height of an object and its mass.)

speed: How fast an object moves. The distance that object travels divided by the time it takes.

velocity: A combination of speed and the direction in which an object travels. [4]

I have found that the second way to experience a roller coaster is just to get on and ride! Thrill seekers travel to amusement parks from all over to experience the roller coaster. The knowledge that comes from experiencing the roller coaster is quite different than the scientific knowledge of the roller coaster. Which knowledge do you have of God?

God never created us to live bored, especially bored of Him. God created us to be so intrigued and fascinated by Him. We were made to experience God and His love in a very real way. In my opinion most people don't experience God in an experiential way; they know all about Him, but they don't really experience Him.

1 John 3:1 (emphasis mine)

"***Behold*** *what manner of* ***love*** *the Father has bestowed* (some translations say lavished) *on us, that we should be called children of God!"*

The word behold in this passage is the Greek word *eidō*. It means to see and know by the senses, to discover and observe, to be skilled in and cherish, to become acquainted with by experientially [5]. The word love in this passage is agapē. Do you know what the word love in that verse means? When it is translated, it means ecstasy and that means "to be out of balance or beside oneself, usually out of a strong joyful emotion [6]."

We are given an invitation to experience often the powerful, joyful ecstasy of God's love that fills our emotions beyond our comprehension. This is the call of God on all His children.

Chapter 2
Acknowledging the Lord

It is not enough to know about God. It is also not enough to sit idle waiting for God to sovereignly move in our life. We are in relationship. We are not in a relationship with the Book; we are in relationship with the Word who became flesh and dwelt among us. If that weren't enough, the finished work of Jesus invites the Father to make His home in us, as well as, the Holy Spirit who leads us and gives to us all the things Jesus purchased for us. "Yah hoo!," I hear you say. This is who we are in relationship with.

In the previous chapter I covered two Greek words about knowledge, and now I would like to cover two Hebrew words about knowledge.

Jeremiah 9:23-24 (emphasis mine)

[23] Thus says the LORD: "Let not the wise man glory in his wisdom, Let not the mighty man glory in his might, Nor let the rich man glory in his riches; [24] But let him who

glories glory in this, That he <u>understands</u> and <u>knows</u> Me, That I am the LORD, exercising lovingkindness, judgment, and righteousness in the earth. For in these I delight," says the Lord."

The word understands in this passage is the Hebrew word "sakal", which speaks to an intellectual comprehension of God [7]. God expects His children to grapple with serious questions and seek serious answers. Thinking deeply is part of following Him. Now we discover that understanding (*sakal*) isn't quite enough. We are also commanded to "know" Him (*yada*). So, what's the difference between these two verbs and why are they both essential?

The intimacy of deep relationship, the friendship, the honesty, the confrontation, the instruction, and the familial bonding are all part of "yada." He's our best friend, our protective parent, our mentor, our examiner, our guide, our lover, our comforter, our doctor, our judge, and a host of other close connections. Understanding who God is not enough.

Understanding who He is *and* experiencing intimacy with Him is the essence of true relationship. Relationship with God is about acknowledging the complete sovereignty of God in life. It is allowing Him to fill life with the "yada" qualities of steadfast faithfulness, justice, and righteousness which He possesses, delights, and desires to find in us. More information will not produce more relationship. I would propose to you that if you do not "know" God relationally (yada) and the "yada" characteristics are *not* routinely expressed in your living, then you do not

understand or know Him.
And of course, I say that in
the loveliest possible way.
God gave us senses and we
are to encounter Him in our
senses. That is what "yada"
alludes to. Relationship
with God is how He defines
it, not us.

Proverbs 3:5-6 is one of my
favorite scriptures that
tends to appear in every
message I preach, and book
I write, in fact, I've already
mentioned it once.

Proverbs 3:5-6 *"Trust in the
Lord with all your heart.
Lean not under your own
understanding. In all your*

ways <u>*acknowledge*</u> *Him, and He will direct your paths."*

The word acknowledge in this passage is the word "yada". Blue letter Bible defines "yada" to mean: to know or to experience, to learn to know, to see, to perceive, to find out and discern, to confess, to be skilled in, to be known, to declare, and to be made known [8]. In all our ways know God, see God, and confess; be skilled in knowing God personally and He will direct our paths. Another way to say it is to reveal yourself personally to God and He will direct your paths.

The direct your path means to make crooked ways straight. The translation literally teaches us how to navigate through difficulty. When things go well, acknowledge Him. When things are difficult, acknowledge Him. In all of our ways we have to find the place of communion with God, because then God gives us the ability to navigate through difficult paths. We never want to throw in the towel or run away from difficulty. But it's our relationship with God that gets us through.

The nature of God in us and our encounter of that nature is what gets us through – it's what directs our paths. When instructing my children in the ways of God, I make things very simple. If it isn't good, it isn't God. We all know God is good but when something isn't good, why do some put God's name on it? The devil has a job description given to him in scripture. It is to rob, kill, steal, and destroy. So, then the opposite is true of God. His nature is to give, protect, and make new. We have an invitation to partake from who God is for us. Acknowledging God is a key for us in unlocking the nature of God in our lives. The nature of God is ours for asking.

We have to start asking good questions. Who, what, when, where, how, and why are the questions. Right out of the gate, we have to understand that God *doesn't* answer the why question. His response will most likely be, "Ask a better question." One of my favorite relational questions ever is, "Who is it that You want to be for me now that You couldn't have been at any other time?" You can also ask, "What am I believing about myself that would cause me to behave this way?" "When" is a timing question. Our timing is important and so is His. We have to ask the Lord "when" questions to be looking for His timing. How about, "Where do you want me to go? Where am I in relation to where I need to be?" Here's another question: "What's really going on here?"

Two of the best questions were asked on the day of Pentecost.
1. What does this mean?
2. What must we do?

When Holy Spirit poured Himself out mightily these two questions appear in verse 12 and 37 of Acts chapter 2. Notice Peter's response in the very next verse 38. I believe this is still Holy Spirit's response: Repent! We have to repent of some of the presuppositions we have about church, knowledge, relationship with God, and the way we approach spirituality.

Chapter 3

Truth is Encountered Not Just Understood

I have grown up and live in the conservative Midwest. Midwest Christian culture tends to be gauged toward serious and stoic. Spirituality is usually frowned upon and avoided because of the risk factor of leaning towards new age theology, or at the very least, not being done "decently and in order." This mentality has robbed us of knowing God. Even our

Old Testament heroes encountered God. Moses for instance knew the <u>ways</u> of God and the nature of God, but the Israelites whom he was leading, were only acquainted with God's <u>acts</u> (Psalms 103:7-8).

Encounter and experience have become dirty words in the church it seems. The fear is that emotionalism is just another "ism" that we have to take authority over and drive it out. Here's the deal – God created our emotions to be healthy and to function under the authority of Jesus. This is healthy. Our emotions

shouldn't be calling the
shots, but they should be
present to either diagnose a
problem or to reward a
good choice.
Righteousness, peace, and
joy feel good.

I have many great friends
and family members that
have reformed theology or
are fundamental in their
understanding of God.
There have been many
conversations I have had
with them in regard to
knowing the God of
encounter. Most spiritual
conversations have been
serious and unproductive. I
hold the humorous motto

that this type of fundamentalism is mainly mental with no fun. It's hard to encounter God when churches demonize encountering God.

The enemy's objective is to steal. He wants to steal our experience and encounters as well as our understanding of God. God's purpose is to give us Christ's fullness in every area of our lives. So, when it comes to our experiencing Christ's fullness in our lives, our feelings and emotions should be engaged in a healthy way just as much as

our understanding as we
encounter God.

It seems we are prone to be
people of two extremes.
The one extreme is being a
person of experience;
following every feeling and
living tossed back and forth
by emotionalism. The other
extreme being an
intellectual – only
embracing what makes
sense to my understanding.
The emotional driven group
tends to label the
intellectual group as
Pharisees. The intellectual
group tends to label the
emotional group as flakes.
The truth is we need the

balance of both truths. We are not following a book; we are following Christ. However, we are not following our emotions. We are led by Christ into truth and feeling good is not the fullness of Christ. PART of Christ's fullness was that He was a Man of sorrow acquainted with grief (Isaiah 53:3). Now He wasn't that entirely, but it was a PART of His experience. So, we don't walk around defeated by sorrow as though we are being Godly, but we don't reject the sorrow of Christ. It seems quite paradoxical, but truth is interpreted in paradox.

Jesus said that we have to die to live. So, does that mean that we are supposed to die? Yes. I thought Jesus came to give us life and not death – He did. So, are we supposed to live life to the full? Yes. Sometimes the key truth is to die and sometimes the key truth is to live.

When it comes to sorrow and joy, it's a truth held in paradox. A paradox is two seemingly conflicting ideas contained in the same truth. When it comes to experience and understanding, feelings and intellectualism, or emotions and principals, we need both sides. They are two sides of the same truth. Don't stop short of Christ's fullness in your life. Which side do you lean towards? The primary truth is that we need to have relationship with God.

One of my friends and I were spending some time together recently. As conversation ebbs and flows I happened to ask Him what God was speaking to him recently. He had a puzzled look on his face as though

he was unsure how to
answer. So, instead of
taking a safe and friendlier
conversational approach, he
took a theological one. He
replied, "God has said all He
has to say in the Bible." I
paused for a moment and
said, "So, what you're saying
is that God spent 4000 years
writing a book and then lost
His voice?" He said, "I
wouldn't put it that way but,
yes." I asked him then what
a relationship with God
looks like for him, and I
noted a few things. First, it
was largely one sided and
the reason being, in his
admission, was largely due

to the sovereignty of God. Second, it was a relationship with the Bible at best, but more accurately a relationship with rules. And lastly, empty and emotionless.

To think God wrote a book and lost his voice or took a vow of silence is a heresy that has cost us our inheritance and relationship with the Father, Son, and Holy Spirit.

Why is it that many Christians have no problem in believing that it's easy to hear the liar – the devil? Why is it that some

Christians believe it's so hard to hear the voice of God? Wouldn't you think that as a believer it would be easier to hear the voice of the Father than the voice of the deceiver? I am confused when I talk to people who believe that as a follower of Christ, it's easier to believe the lie than it is to believe the truth. We need to get our story straight! If we spent the rest of our life inventorying what we have in Christ through the Holy Spirit, we would never be in lack.

How do you have fullness of joy in the same place of

anger? Either His wrath was satisfied in Christ or it wasn't. God was happy to sacrifice Jesus for the payment of sin and for the judgement of humanity. In Christ, the Father has accepted us, and He is absolutely pleased with our position in Jesus. So, the question becomes: is God happy with Jesus? If we are in Christ, God's pleasure is with us (Proverbs 8:31). Growing up in the church, I've heard many messages about sorrow, but few on joy and healthy emotions. Why?

I want to illustrate encounter by using the

scripture coupled with experience on just the subject of joy. Joy is such a big deal because it's hard to have relationship, or it's hard to want a relationship with someone who's angry and disillusioned with who you are. The only one disillusioned with who we are in Christ is us. God has never had an illusion about who we are or who we are not. He is crystal clear about who we are in Jesus. We are the ones discovering the brilliance and wonder of our new nature in Christ. This is a source of extreme joy!

The fruits of the Spirit are to be enjoyed not studied. The joy of the Lord is a life changer, not a bible study that we put in the drawer and carry on our life without it. There is only one acceptable level of joy and that is full (John 16:24). What then does the fullness of joy look like in our lives? If in His presence is fullness of joy, I'm trying to figure out why some people think He's mad or in a bad mood. I think for some of us, our face needs to get the message of God's fullness of joy.

In Numbers 6 Aaron prays that the Lord would lift up

the light of His countenance upon us. I believe that is the best way of saying that God is happy and that He is a smiler, and specifically He is smiling at you! What would our lives look like if we lived them under the experience of God smiling on us?

Our circumstances in life do not dictate what level of joy we walk in. So, how much joy do you manifest in your life? We can choose joy no matter what. The question is how can we choose joy when we don't feel like being joyful? Well, first of all, we are not feelers; we are believers. If we wait on our feelings to get joy, we'll

only have joy in seasons If
we believe for joy, we'll
have it all the time.

Rejoicing is the highway of
that joy comes through.
Rejoicing is a choice, joy is
the outcome. What does it
mean to rejoice? The word
means to exult. When we
focus on how wonderful the
Lord is and get into position
with His goodness, we are
rejoicing. Rejoicing releases
the joy of the Lord. The joy
of the Lord is to be
experienced! Rejoicing is
our response to His joy. Of
all the promises we have as
Christians, our access to joy
may be the greatest promise
and encounter. Joy is

supernatural. We can't
produce joy apart from the
Spirit. Joy is a fruit of the
Spirit. Rejoicing is a choice;
joy is the outcome.

We need to understand that
God is not passive about Joy
in the life of believers. He
requires it; it's a big deal to
God. It's big to Him because
we reflect Jesus.

If you're not naturally
happy, act like you are. You
might say, *"I don't want to
be phony,"* I'd suggest you
try. God wants you to be
the happiest person in your
city. We need to work with
the Holy Spirit to receive
more joy in our life. We

need to work at smiling. We
need to practice the art of
belly laughing. He is the
happiest person I know.
He's the most positive,
enthusiastic, charismatic,
energetic, and wonderful
person that I have ever met
or encountered in my entire
life. My encounter with His
happiness has sustained me.
When I look back over my
life, the one thing that
pulled me through hellish
circumstances was the
happiness of God and the
manifestation of
supernatural joy in the Holy
Spirit.

We need to face everything
with joy in our heart. We

need to fight to be filled
with Joy. Joy is a weapon
against the enemy. James
tells us to count it all joy
when we face trials. What's
he saying? Do the math.
When we face trials with joy
in our heart is pays us
dividends. In fact, if you
finish that verse you'll find
that we'll be perfect lacking
nothing. Nehemiah 8:10
says, *"The joy of the LORD is
your strength."* The enemy
seeks to keep you unhappy
and miserable. Sometimes
we get into hard
circumstances, and the first
thing that happens is our joy
is lost. That's not right.
When everything is working
against us, joy propels us to

another level. Joy should never be lost in our circumstances; it releases us into higher levels of faith. Joy teaches us how to live and abide in the presence of God.

What if joy is the catalyst to what takes you from your problem to the promise of all things work for good to those who love God and are called according to His purposes? What if joy could take you into a place with God where faith could rise rather than unbelief, doubt, and fear? What if joy was the cure for unbelief, doubt, and fear?

Joy can't exist in the same place at the same time as anxiety. One of them has to go; you get to choose. We don't need things to change to be happy. What if joy just changes us? Joy is everlasting (Isaiah 61:7). Everlasting joy is not for after we die; it's talking about the moment we got saved. The moment we got saved, we began eternal life and stepped into abundant life (John 10:10).

Think back to when you got saved up until now. Ask yourself, "Have I been robbed of joy and from processing everything in life through the delight of

God?" If the answer is yes, it's time for an encounter with joy. Joy is the cure for negativity. Some of us are so conditioned to be miserable we don't even know that we are anymore.

If joy were not enough, pair it with gladness (Psalm 21:6). Pair longsuffering with joy (Colossians 1:10-11 & Psalms 126:5). Joy goes good with just about anything. An encounter with joy will transform you forever!

Joy can be obnoxious to people who don't have it. I use to hate it when people would laugh in the spirit. I

thought it was so rude. I
remember the Holy Spirit
spoke to me about this and
said, "Let me get this
straight; you are upset
about people being happy
and laughing, and you think
there is something wrong
with them?" I know, it's as
dumb as it sounds. Now I
think it's contagiously
wonderful! So, I repented
and the encounters I've had
in joy have been
inexpressible and full of
glory (1 Peter 1:8)!

God wants to see you
laughing and enjoying your
life. God wants to see you
laughing at the enemy
(Psalm 37:12-13). No

wonder Paul said, *"Rejoice in the Lord always and again I say rejoice."* Treat yourself to a double portion of Joy – you deserve it!

What if there was like ninety percent more joy in your life than you are experiencing right now? What is the level of your joy right now? What are the things in your life right now that could use a heavy dose of laughter? What if joy is one of the needs you get met in Christ Jesus? What if joy releases you into faith – into a higher level of relationship to God? What is it that has been set aside in the Spirit that can only be accessed through

Joy? When is the last time
you went to church and sat
during worship and just took
pleasure in the happiness of
God? What if joy is in you
right now and you just need
to let it out? What if joy is
the avenue to a greater
understanding of the love of
God? What is standing
between you and rejoicing
as a lifestyle? What would it
take for you to travel with
more joy? What would it
take for you view everything
with a positive outlook?
What would it take for you
to learn to live in the delight
that God has for you? What
would you say to being
transformed by joy? What

is stopping you from that encounter?

Joy is a choice we make. There's a reason that there are so many scriptures that concern joy. Joy is just one of the thousands of encounters that we have available for us. The Bible itself should be viewed as a book of encounters that are available for us to have. Joy is the doorway for many other encounters.

Many want the result of joy without processing joy in their life. Joy isn't dispensational; it's foundational!

Chapter 3

The Mind of Christ

There is an inseparable link
between experience and
understanding. The bottom
line is that truth needs to be
encountered because truth
was meant to work for us.
Language is so important to
passing on what God has
given us through encounter
because it paves the way for
others to inquire of God to
do the same thing for them
as He has for us. Our
instruction should never be
done with words only. It

should be accompanied with the Holy Spirit's power so that the fullness of the gospel doesn't rest on the ability of persuasive words but rather on the power of God (1 Corinthians 2:1-5).

The power of God is contained in our experiential not factual knowledge. The power of God is in our relational exchange with Him. In this book I have gone over many different words and ideas concerning Biblically defined knowledge, yet I still do not feel as though I have exhausted the subject. I shared about ginosko earlier in this reading, I also shared about eidō. The question is: what are the similarities and the differences in the meaning of these two words "to know"? The similarities are that both forms of knowledge expressed here are verbs and are about experience, not intellectual knowledge. The difference is interesting.

Eidō, Ginosko, & Epiginosko

Ginosko indicates a relationship between the person "knowing" and the object known. In this respect, what is "known" is of value or importance to the one who knows, and hence, priority of experiencing relationship is implied. Ginosko "knowledge" is obtained, not by intellectual activity, but by the operation of Holy Spirit. The verb is also used to convey the thought of connection or union, as between man and woman, (Matthew 1:25 & Luke 1:34).

Eidō means to have Divine knowledge of something. Ginosko suggests a progression in "knowledge," while eidō suggests fullness of "knowledge. Ginosko implies an active relationship between the one who "knows" and the person or thing "known"; eidō expresses the fact that the object has simply come within the scope of the "knower's" perception. So, in other words, we get perfected in our knowledge or experience of God (eidō) because of our growing knowledge or experience (ginosko). The regular encounters we have in relationship with Him are the life and growth of who we are. We are in Christ, learning to become Christ-like. We are in fullness already but we are learning to encounter and know what fullness is.

The next word I would like to share is the word epiginosko. Epiginosko suggests advanced "knowledge" or special appreciation – meaning "knowing full well." Epiginosko implies a special participation in the person "known", and gives greater weight to the knowledge known in a relational exchange [9].

The Triune Nature of Knowing

Eidō is brought in from external sources. Ginosko is brought into being by the understanding of the soul. Epiginosko is the knowledge of the Spirit - that life changing knowledge that can only be known by the enlightening presence of Holy Spirit within.

Another way to view the three ways of knowing is that eidō is to know intuitively – it is knowledge perceived immediately and requiring no application of reason. Ginosko is to know experientially – it is knowledge gained by trial and practice. Epiginosko takes the experiential knowledge of ginosko a step further; the thing becoming so known as to cause profound change in the one who knows it. It is the knowledge so fully participated in, that it can change my life.

Knowledge and Wisdom

1 Corinthians 2:6-8 says,
"*However, we speak wisdom among those who are mature, yet not the wisdom of this age, nor of the rulers of this age, who are coming to nothing. [7] But we speak the wisdom of God in a mystery, the hidden wisdom which God ordained before the ages for our glory, [8] which none of the rulers of this age knew; for had they known, they would not have crucified the Lord of glory.*"

Wisdom is the marriage of encounter and understanding. Wisdom isn't being smart; it is knowing how God would think about something in a particular circumstance. How would we know that? It is because of our growth in relationship with His nature and His truth. Let's face it, the Pharisees were the ones who knew the scriptures, but when the Word stood in their midst they sought to destroy Him. They had factual knowledge with no relationship. They had a form of Godliness with no power.

Having The Mind of Christ

1 Corinthians 2:9 says, *"Eye has not seen, nor ear heard,*

nor have entered into the heart of man the things which God has prepared for those who love Him." Many have interpreted that to mean when we die we get an awesome mansion with a great reward. At the very least, many have the idea that there is no way that we can ever know what God has prepared for us who love Him. The next verse blows that idea right out of the water.

1 Corinthians 2:10-12 says, *"But God has revealed <u>them</u>* (the things eye has not seen nor ear heard) *to us through His Spirit. For the Spirit searches all things, yes, the*

deep things of God. [11] For what man knows the things of a man except the spirit of the man which is in him? Even so no one knows the things of God except the Spirit of God. [12] Now we have received, not the spirit of the world, but the Spirit who is from God, that we might know the things that have been freely given to us by God."

This tells us that God reveals the things that eye has not seen nor ear heard. God reveals them in relationship as we see perfectly through relational growth and encounter.

This passage goes on to say that, *"<u>These things</u> (which eye hasn't seen nor ear heard, but we know relationally) we also speak, not in words which man's wisdom teaches but which the Holy Spirit teaches, comparing spiritual things with spiritual. [14] But the natural man does not receive the things of the Spirit of God, for they are foolishness to him; nor can he <u>know</u> them, because they are spiritually discerned. [15] But he who is spiritual judges all things, yet he himself is rightly judged by no one. [16] For "who has <u>known</u> the mind of the LORD that he may instruct Him?"*

But we have the mind of Christ."

Only the mind of Christ would know how to know Christ. Only the mind of Christ would contain the perfect knowledge of His fullness. Only the mind of Christ could teach us to see and hear and be known. Only the mind of Christ could discern all things spiritual. Only the mind of Christ could hold the wisdom, instruction, and understanding of God. Thank God we have the mind of Christ!

Chapter 4
Taking the Next Step

Our test to receiving any truth involves vulnerability, honesty, and wisdom. How do we make the change that God is inviting us into?
What are the first steps to living out this relational approach?

My encouragement would be to stay curious, humble, and seek to experience the Lord. The hesitation for most of us is that we don't want to be deceived or led astray. The Holy Spirit <u>will</u>

lead us into all truth, and He is very good at His role of disclosing to us what we need, when we need it.

Suspicion is not helpful in our quest for truth. The nature of new experience with the Lord is that we may have to be open to receive something different. The vulnerability required for this has the potential to be both intimidating and rewarding. This is where trust comes into play.

Our intentionality and faithfulness to the Lord will be rewarded. The Lord sees our diligence and desires that we sincerely know Him.

He is the rewarder of those
who diligently seek Him!
(Hebrews 11:6)

Spiritual hunger is created
by feeding. In the natural,
hunger is the result of lack
of food – but in the Spirit,
hunger is the result of
feeding on Spiritual food.
Jesus said those who hunger
will be filled, but when we
are filled, we want more.
This is how we enlarge.

Tragically some stop short of
a relational experience with
the Lord because they are
content with living with
factual study of the Bible. Is
your current theology
threatened by the love of

God? What is your level of
hunger? Are you open to
something new? Are you
seeking something
profound, or are you
satisfied to level off? Is
encounter on your radar?
What are you asking and
believing God for? Does
something different to you
mean that it's unbiblical? Is
the Holy Spirit leading you
into something different
right now? Does your heart
burn inside of you when you
read this book?

If we are willing to sharpen
our focus, wait quietly
before the Lord, and quiet
ourselves – encounters are
waiting for us.

Another tool I've used in the past to initiate encounter is to hang around people who believe God for encounter as well. I love attending conferences, church prayer meetings, worship services, and small group studies where people have gathered in the Name of Jesus with the express purpose of experiencing God. I have found that worship is a profound key. When is the last time you upgraded your worship? Are you constantly filling your time with teaching and study or are you giving equal time for worship and prayer? There have been times in my life where upgrading my worship has taken preeminence and so my focus gets refined to what Holy Spirit wants to pour into my life.

Jesus taught that when we drink of the water He gives us, we will thirst no more (John 4). Does this principal teach that we are not to long for something more from our relationship with Jesus, or does it teach that as we experience this encounter with Jesus, out of that will come many more wonderful satisfying times of refreshment? I would propose the latter.

God can sovereignly orchestrate an encounter in His providence, but it's His will that we live a life of experiencing Him.

The glad tidings of great joy is that God loves to be close to us and wants us to know Him better. If you long to experience more of God's presence, you can take steps that will lead you closer to Him, inviting him to make His presence known more strongly in your life.

I encourage you to choose adventure over safety, and accept the fact that there is nothing safe about pursuing God. Decide to take whatever risks you need to take in order to experience the blessing of getting closer to God. Be willing to have God turn your life upside down, reshape your values and redirect your energy. Rather than trying to stay inside your comfort zones, be open to saying "yes" to God whenever He calls you to follow him on adventures. Expect encounters with God that inspire awe and wonder in you.

Pursue revival by learning about past moves of God and finding out how and where God is moving in the earth.

Supernatural encounters with God aren't actually rare; God manifests His presence in tangible ways every day to various people on Earth. So expect to encounter God in a way that you can powerfully sense.

Be confident in approaching God (Hebrews 4:16). Let go of whatever is distracting you from giving God your full attention. Remove distractions from your life so you can experience God to the fullest.

God's presence is for us to enjoy and to inspire us to open ourselves up in deeper ways to the Holy Spirit's

ongoing work of
transformation!

I hope this reading has
challenged you to get
outside the box of your own
understanding and reach for
more!

End Notes

[1] "G1108 - gnōsis - Strong's Greek Lexicon (NKJV)." Blue Letter Bible. Web. 28 Sep, 2017. <https://www.blueletterbibl e.org//lang/lexicon/lexicon. cfm?Strongs=G1108&t=NKJ V>.

[2] "G1922 - epignōsis - Strong's Greek Lexicon (NKJV)." Blue Letter Bible. Web. 28 Sep, 2017. <https://www.blueletterbibl e.org//lang/lexicon/lexicon. cfm?Strongs=G1922&t=NKJ V>.

[3] "G1097 - ginōskō - Strong's Greek Lexicon (NKJV)." Blue Letter Bible. Web. 28 Sep, 2017. <https://www.blueletterbibl e.org//lang/lexicon/lexicon. cfm?Strongs=G1097&t=NKJ V>.

[4] "Lesson: Physics of Roller Coasters." Contributed by: Engineering K-PhD Program,

Pratt School of Engineering,
Duke University.
26 April 2017. Web.
https://www.teachengineeri
ng.org/lessons/view/duk_ro
llercoaster_music_less

[5] "G1492 - eidō - Strong's
Greek Lexicon (NKJV)." Blue
Letter Bible. Web. 28 Sep,
2017.
<https://www.blueletterbibl
e.org//lang/lexicon/lexicon.
cfm?Strongs=G1492&t=NKJ
V>.

[6] "G26 - agapē - Strong's
Greek Lexicon (NKJV)." Blue
Letter Bible. Web. 28 Sep,
2017.
<https://www.blueletterbibl

e.org//lang/lexicon/lexicon.
cfm?Strongs=G26&t=NKJV>.

[7] "H7919 - sakal - Strong's
Hebrew Lexicon (NKJV)."
Blue Letter Bible. Web. 28
Sep, 2017.
<https://www.blueletterbibl
e.org//lang/lexicon/lexicon.
cfm?Strongs=H7919&t=NKJ
V>.

[8] "H3045 - yada` - Strong's
Hebrew Lexicon (NKJV)."
Blue Letter Bible. Web. 28
Sep, 2017.
<https://www.blueletterbibl
e.org//lang/lexicon/lexicon.
cfm?Strongs=H3045&t=NKJ
V>.

[9] "G1921 - epiginōskō - Strong's Greek Lexicon (NKJV)." Blue Letter Bible. Web. 28 Sep, 2017. <https://www.blueletterbibl e.org//lang/lexicon/lexicon. cfm?Strongs=G1921&t=NKJ V>.

Other Books from Sword of the Spirit Publishing

Knowing Who We Are: Discovering Our True Identities in Christ by Mark Calvin Nelson

Finding My Heavenly Father by Jeff Reuter

Saved Twice by Andy Peterson and Donald James Parker

Will the Real Christianity Please Stand Up by Donald James Parker

Old Rugged Cross by Donald James Parker

The Accidental Missionary by Chip Rossetti and Donald James Parker

Feature Movies from

Sword of the Spirit Publishing

Gramps Goes to College

In Gramps' Shoes

The Unexpected Bar Mitzvah

Love Waits

Best Friends Eternally

Best Friends Recycled

Best Friend Genetically Modified

Mission Improbable

Old Rugged Cross

www.ingramcontent.com/pod-product-compliance
Lightning Source LLC
Chambersburg PA
CBHW071819020426
42331CB00007B/1552